REPORT of Mr W. E. CORMACK'S Journey
in search of the Red Indians in Newfoundland.

W. E. CORMACK

[ZHINGOORA BOOKS]

This edition is published by
Zhingoora Books.

The Cover is Designed by Pallav Sethiya.

REPORT of Mr W. E. CORMACK'S Journey in search of the Red Indians in Newfoundland.

Read before the Boeothick Institution at St John's, Newfoundland.

From the Edinburgh New Philosophical Journal.

PURSUANT to special summons, a meeting of this Institution was held at St John's on the 12th day of January 1828; the Honourable A.W. Desbarres, Vice-Patron, in the chair. The Honourable Chairman stated, that the primary motive which led to the formation of the Institution, was the desire of opening a communication with, and promoting the civilization of, the Red Indians of Newfoundland; and of procuring, if possible, an authentic history of that unhappy race of people, in order that their language, customs and pursuits, might be contrasted with those of other tribes of Indians and nations;—that, in following up the chief object of the institution, it was anticipated that much information would be obtained respecting the natural productions of the island; the interior of which is less known than any other of the British possessions abroad. Their excellent President, keeping all these objects in view, had permitted nothing worthy of research to escape his scrutiny, and consequently a very wide field of information was now introduced to their notice, all apparently highly interesting and useful to society, if properly cultivated. He was aware of their very natural anxiety to hear from the president an outline of his recent expedition, and he would occupy their attention farther, only by observing, that the purposes of the present meeting would be best accomplished by taking into consideration the different subjects recommended to them in the president's report, and passing such resolutions as might be considered necessary to govern the future proceedings of the Institution.

The President, W.E. Cormack, Esq. then laid the following Statement before the meeting.

Having so recently returned, I will now only lay before you a brief outline of my expedition in search of the Boeothicks or Red Indians, confining my remarks exclusively to its primary object. A detailed report of the journey will be prepared, and submitted to the Institution, whenever I shall have leisure to arrange the other interesting materials which have been collected.

My party consisted of three Indians, whom I procured from among the other different tribes, viz. an intelligent and able man of the Abenakie tribe, from Canada; an elderly Mountaineer from Labrador; and an adventurous young Micmack, a native of this island, together with myself. It was difficult to obtain men fit for the purpose, and the trouble attending on this prevented my entering on the expedition a month earlier in the season. It was my intention to have commenced our search at White Bay, which is nearer the northern extremity of the island than where we did, and to have travelled southward; but the weather not permitting to carry my party thither by water, after several days delay, I unwillingly changed my line of route.

On the 31st of October 1828 [Sic: 30th of October 1827] last, we entered the country at the mouth of the River Exploits, on the north side, at what is called the Northern Arm. We took a north-westerly direction to lead us to Hall's Bay, which place we reached through an almost uninterrupted forest, over a hilly country, in eight days. This tract comprehends the country interior from New Bay, Badger Bay, Seal Bay, &c.; these being minor bays, included in Green or Notre Dame Bay, at the north-east part of the island, and well known to have been always heretofore the summer residence of the Red Indians.

On the fourth day after our departure, at the east end of Badger Bay-Great Lake, at a *portage* known by the name of the Indian Path, we found traces made by the Red Indians, evidently in the spring or summer of the preceding year. Their party had had two canoes; and here was a *canoe-rest,* on which the daubs of red-ochre, and the roots of trees used to fasten or tie it together appeared fresh. A canoe-rest is simply a few beams, supported horizontally, about five feet from the ground, by perpendicular posts. A party with two canoes, when descending from the interior to the sea-coast, through such a part of the country as this, where there are troublesome portages, leave one canoe resting, bottom up, on this kind of frame, to protect it from injury by the weather, until their return. Among other things which lay strewed about here, were a spear-shaft, eight feet in length, recently made and ochred; parts of old canoes, fragments of their skin-dresses, &c. For some distance around, the trunks of many of the birch, and of that species of spruce pine called here the Var (*Pinus balsamifera*), had been rinded; these people using the inner part of the bark of that kind of tree for food. Some of the cuts in the trees with the axe were evidently made the preceding year. Besides these, we were elated by other encouraging signs. The traces left by the Red Indians are so peculiar, that we were confident those we saw here were made by them.

This spot has been a favourite place of settlement with these people. It is situated at the commencement of a *portage*, which forms a communication by a path between the sea-coast at Badger Bay, about eight miles to the north-east, and a chain of lakes extending westerly and southerly from hence, and discharging themselves by a rivulet into the

River Exploits, about thirty miles from its mouth. A path also leads from this place to the lakes, near New Bay, to the eastward. Here are the remains of one of their villages, where the vestiges of eight or ten winter *mamateeks* or wigwams, each intended to contain from six to eighteen or twenty people, are distinctly seen close together. Besides these, there are the remains of a number of summer wigwams. Every winter wigwam has close by it a small square-mouthed or oblong pit, dug into the earth, about four feet deep, to preserve their stores, &c. in. Some of these pits were lined with birch-rind. We discovered also in this village the remains of a vapour-bath. The method used by the Boeothicks to raise the steam, was by pouring water on large stones, made very hot for the purpose, in the open air, by burning a quantity of wood around them; after this process, the ashes were removed, and a hemispherical frame-work, closely covered with skins, to exclude the external air, was fixed over the stones. The patient then crept in under the skins, taking with him a birch-rind-bucket of water, and a small bark-dish to dip it out, which, by pouring on the stones, enabled him to raise the steam at pleasure.*

At Hall's Bay we got no useful information from the three (and the only) English families settled there. Indeed we could hardly have expected any; for these, and such people, have been the unchecked and ruthless destroyers of the tribe, the remnant of which we were in search of. After sleeping one night in a *house*, we again struck into the country to the westward.

In five days we were on the high lands south of White Bay, and in sight of the high lands east of the Bay of Islands, on the west coast of Newfoundland. The country south and west of us was low and flat, consisting of marshes, extending in a southerly direction more than thirty miles. In this direction lies the famous Red Indians' Lake. It was now near the middle of November, and the winter had commenced pretty severely in the interior. The country was everywhere covered with snow, and, for some days past, we had walked over the small ponds on the ice. The summits of the hills on which we stood had snow on them, in some places many feet deep. The deer were migrating from the rugged and dreary mountains in the north to the low mossy barrens and more woody parts in the south; and we inferred, that if any of the Red Indians had been at White Bay during the past summer, they might be at that time stationed about the borders of the low tract of country before us, at the *deer-passes*, or were employed somewhere else in the interior, killing deer for winter provision. At these passes, which are particular places in the migration lines of path, such as the extreme ends of, and straights in, many of the large lakes,—the foot of valleys between high or rugged mountains,—fords in the large rivers, and the like,—the Indians kill great numbers of deer with very little trouble, during their migrations. We looked out for two days from the summits of the hills adjacent, trying to discover the smoke from the camps of the Red Indians; but in vain. These hills command a very extensive view of the country in every direction.

* Since my return, I learn from the captive Red Indian woman *Shawnawdithit,* that the vapour-bath is chiefly used by old people, and for rheumatic affections.

Shanawdithit is the survivor of three Red Indian females, who were taken by, or rather who gave themselves up, exhausted with hunger, to some English furriers, about five years ago, in Notre Dame Bay. She is the only one of that tribe in the hands of the English, and the only one that has ever lived so long among them. It appears extraordinary, and it is to be regretted, that this woman has not been taken care of, nor noticed before, in a manner which the peculiar and interesting circumstances connected with her tribe and herself would have led us to expect.

We now determined to proceed towards the Red Indians' Lake, sanguine that, at that known rendezvous, we would find the objects of our search.

Travelling over such a country, except when winter has fairly set in, is truly laborious.

In about ten days we got a glimpse of this beautifully majestic and splendid sheet of water. The ravages of fire, which we saw in the woods for the last two days, indicated that man had been near. We looked down on the lake, from the hills at the northern extremity, with feelings of anxiety and admiration:—No canoe could be discovered moving on its placid surface in the distance. We were the first Europeans who had seen it in an unfrozen state, for the three former parties who had visited it before, were here in the winter, when its waters were frozen and covered over with snow. They had reached it from below, by way of the River Exploits, on the ice. We approached the lake with hope and caution; but found to our mortification that the Red Indians had deserted it for some years past. My party had been so excited, so sanguine, and so determined to obtain an interview of some kind with these people, that, on discovering, from appearances every where around us, that the Red Indians—the terror of the Europeans as well as the other Indian inhabitants of Newfoundland—no longer existed, the spirits of one and all of us were very deeply affected. The old mountaineer was particularly overcome. There were every where indications that this had long been the central and undisturbed rendezvous of the tribe, where they had enjoyed peace and security. But these primitive people had abandoned it, after having been tormented by parties of Europeans during the last eighteen [Sic: thirteen] years. Fatal rencounters had on these occasions unfortunately taken place.

We spent several melancholy days wandering on the borders of the east end of the lake, surveying the various remains of what we now contemplated to have been an unoffending and cruelly extirpated people. At several places, by the margin of the lake, are small clusters of winter and summer wigwams in ruins. One difference, among others, between the Boeothick wigwams and those of the other Indians is, that in most of the former there are small hollows, like nests, dug in the earth around the fire-place, one for each person to sit in. These hollows are generally so close together, and also so close to the fire-place, and to the sides of the wigwam, that I think it probable these people have been accustomed to sleep in a sitting position. There was one wooden building constructed for drying and smoking venison in, still perfect; also a small log-house, in a dilapidated condition, which we took to have been once a store-house. The wreck of a large handsome birch-rind canoe, about twenty-two feet in length, comparatively new, and certainly very little used, lay thrown up among the bushes at the beach. We supposed that the violence of a storm had rent it in the way it was found, and that the people who were in it had perished; for the iron nails, of which there was no want, all remained in it. Had there been any survivors, nails being much prized by these people, they never having held intercourse with

Europeans, such an article would most likely have been taken out for use again. All the birch trees in the vicinity of the lake had been rinded, and many of them and of the spruce fir or var (*Pinus balsamifera*, Canadian balsam tree) had the bark taken off, to use the inner part of it for food, as noticed before.

Their wooden repositories for the dead are what are in the most perfect state of preservation. These are of different constructions, it would appear, according to the character or rank of the persons entombed. In one of them, which resembled a hut, ten feet by eight or nine, and four or five feet high in the centre, floored with squared poles, the roof covered with rinds of trees, and in every way well secured against the weather inside and the intrusion of wild beasts, there were two grown persons laid out at full length on the floor, the bodies wrapped round with deer-skins. One of these bodies appeared to have been placed here not longer ago than five or six years. We thought there were children laid in here also. On first opening this building, by removing the posts which formed the ends, our curiosity was raised to the highest pitch; but what added to our surprise, was the discovery of a white deal coffin, containing a skeleton neatly shrouded in white muslin. After a long pause of conjecture how such a thing existed here, the idea of Mary March occurred to one of the party, and the whole mystery was at once explained.*

* It should be remarked here, that Mary March, so called from the name of the month in which she was taken, was the Red Indian female who was captured and carried away by force from this place by an armed party of English people, nine or ten in number, who came up here in the month of March 1809.[Sic: 1819] The local government authorities at that time did not foresee the result of offering a reward to *bring a Red Indian to them*. Her husband was cruelly shot, after nobly making several attempts, single-handed, to rescue her from the captors, in defiance of their fire-arms and fixed bayonets. His tribe built this cemetery for him, on the foundation of his own wigwam, and his body is one of those now in it. The following winter, Captain Buchan was sent to the River Exploits, by order of the local government of Newfoundland, to take back this woman to the lake where she was captured, and, if possible, at the same time, to open a friendly intercourse with her tribe. But she died on board Captain B.'s vessel, at the mouth of the river. Captain B., however, took up her body to the lake; and not meeting with any of her people, left it where they were afterwards likely to meet with it. It appears the Indians were this winter encamped on the banks of the River Exploits, and observed Captain B.'s party passing up the river on the ice. They retired from their encampments in consequence; and, some weeks afterwards, went by a circuitous route to the lake, to ascertain what the party had been doing there. They found Mary March's body, and removed it from where

Captain B. had left it to where it now lies, by the side of her husband.

With the exception of Captain Buchan's first expedition, by order of the local government of Newfoundland, in the winter of 1810, [Sic: 1815] to endeavour to open a friendly intercourse with the Red Indians, the two parties just mentioned are the only two we know of that had ever before been up to the Red Indian Lake. Captain B. at that time succeeded in forcing an interview with the principal encampment of these people. All of the tribe that remained at that period were then at the Great Lake, divided into parties, and in their winter encampments, at different places in the woods on the margin of the lake. Hostages were exchanged; but Captain B. had not been absent from the Indians two hours, in his return to a depot left by him at a short distance down the river, to take up additional presents for them, when the want of confidence of these people in the whites evinced itself. A suspicion spread among them that he had gone down to bring up a reinforcement of men to take them all prisoners to the sea-coast; and they resolved immediately to break up their encampment and retire farther into the country, and alarm and join the rest of their tribe, who were all at the western parts of the lake. To prevent their proceedings being known, they killed and then cut off the heads of the two English hostages; and, on the same afternoon on which Captain B. had left them, they were in full retreat across the lake, with baggage, children, &c. The whole of them afterwards spent the remainder of the winter together, at a place twenty to thirty miles to the south-west, on the south-east side of the lake. On Captain B.'s return to the lake next day or the day after, the cause of the scene there was inexplicable; and it remained a mystery until now, when we can gather some facts relating to these people from the Red Indian woman *Shawnawdithit*.

In this cemetery were deposited a variety of articles, in some instances the property, in others the representations of the property and utensils, and of the achievements, of the deceased. There were two small wooden images of a man and woman, no doubt meant to represent husband and wife; a small doll, which we supposed to represent a child (for *Mary March* had to leave her only child here, which died two days after she was taken): several small models of their canoes; two small models of boats; an iron axe; a bow and quiver of arrows were placed by the side of *Mary March's* husband; and two fire-stones (radiated iron pyrites, from which they produce fire, by striking them together) lay at his head; there were also various kinds of culinary utensils, neatly made, of birch-rind, and ornamented; and many other things, of some of which we did not know the use or meaning.

Another mode of sepulture which we saw here was, where the body of the deceased had been wrapped in birch rind, and with his property, placed on a sort of scaffold about four feet and a-half from the ground. The scaffold was formed of four posts, about seven feet high, fixed perpendicularly in the ground, to sustain a kind of crib, five feet and a-half in length by four in breadth, with a floor made of small squared beams, laid close together horizontally, and on which the body and property rested.

A third mode was, when the body, bent together, and wrapped in birch-rind, was enclosed in a kind of box on the ground. The box was made of small squared posts, laid on each other horizontally, and notched at the corners, to make them meet close; it was about four feet by three, and two and a-half feet deep, and well lined with birch-rind, to exclude the weather from the inside. The body lay on its right side.

A fourth, and the most common mode of burying among these people, has been, to wrap the body in birch-rind, and cover it over with a heap of stones, on the surface of the earth, in some retired spot; sometimes the body, thus wrapped up, is put a foot or two under the surface, and the spot covered with stones; in one place, where the ground was sandy and soft, they appeared to have been buried deeper, and no stones placed over the graves.

These people appear to have always shewn great respect for their dead; and the most remarkable remains of them commonly observed by Europeans, at the sea-coast, are their burying-places. These are at particular chosen spots; and it is well known that they have been in the habit of bringing their dead from a distance to them. With their women, they bury only their clothes.

On the north side of the lake, opposite the River Exploits, are the extremities of two deer fences, about half a mile apart, where they lead to the water. It is understood that they diverge many miles in north-westerly directions. The Red Indians make these fences to lead and scare the deer to the lake, during the periodical migration of these animals; the Indians being stationed looking out, when the deer get into the water to swim across, the lake being narrow at this end, they attack and kill the animals with spears out of their canoes. In this way they secure their winter provisions before the severity of that season sets in.

There were other old remains of different kinds peculiar to these people met with about the lake.

One night we encamped on the foundation of an old Red Indian wigwam, on the extremity of a point of land which juts out into the lake, and exposed to the view of the whole country around. A large fire at night is the life and soul of such a party as ours, and when it blazed up at times, I could not help observing, that two of my Indians evinced uneasiness and want of confidence in things around, as if they thought themselves usurpers on the Red Indian territory. From time immemorial none of the Indians of the other tribes had ever encamped near this lake fearlessly, and, as we had now done, in the very centre of such a country; the lake and territory adjacent having been always considered to belong exclusively to the Red Indians, and to have been occupied by them. It had been our invariable practice hitherto to encamp near hills, and be on their summits by the dawn of day, to try to discover the morning smoke ascending from the Red Indians' camps; and, to prevent the discovery of ourselves, we extinguished our own fire always some length of time before day-light.

Our only and frail hope now left of seeing the Red Indians lay on the banks of the River Exploits, on our return to the sea-coast.

The Red Indians' Lake discharges itself about three or four miles from its north-east end, and its waters from the River Exploits. From the lake to the sea-coast is considered about seventy miles; and down this noble river the steady perseverance and intrepidity of my Indians carried me on rafts in four days, to accomplish which otherwise, would have required, probably, two weeks. We landed at various places on both banks of the river on our way down, but found no traces of the Red Indians so recent as those seen at the portage at Badger Bay-Great Lake, towards the beginning of our excursion. During our descent, we had to construct new rafts at the different waterfalls. Sometimes we were carried down the rapids at the rate of ten miles an hour or more, with considerable risk of destruction to the whole party, for we were always together on one raft.

What arrests the attention most while gliding down the stream, is the extent of the Indian fences to entrap the deer. They extend from the lake downwards, continuous, on the banks of the river at least thirty miles. There are openings left here and there in them, for the animals to go through and swim across the river, and at these places the Indians are stationed, and kill them in the water with spears, out of their canoes, as at the lake. Here, then, connecting these fences with those on the north-west side of the lake, is at least forty miles of country, easterly and westerly, prepared to intercept all the deer that pass that way in their periodical migrations. It was melancholy to contemplate the gigantic, yet feeble efforts of a whole primitive nation, in their anxiety to provide subsistence, forsaken and going to decay.

There must have been hundreds of the Red Indians, and that not many years ago, to have kept up these fences and ponds. As their numbers were lessened so was their ability to keep them up for the purposes intended; and now the deer pass the whole line unmolested.

We infer, that the few of these people who yet survive, have taken refuge in some sequestered spot, still in the northern part of the island, and where they can procure deer to subsist on.

On the 29th November we were again returned to the mouth of the River Exploits, in thirty days after our departure from thence, after having made a complete circuit of about 200 miles in the Red Indian territory.

*　　*　　*　　*　　*

I have now stated generally the result of my excursion, avoiding, for the present, entering into any detail. The materials collected on this, as well as on my excursion across the interior a few years ago, and on other occasions, put me in possession of a general knowledge of the natural condition and productions of Newfoundland; and, as a member of an institution formed to protect the aboriginal inhabitants of the country in which we live, and to prosecute inquiry into the moral character of man in his primitive state, I can, at this early stage of our institution, assert, trusting to nothing vague, that we already possess more information concerning these people than has been obtained during the two centuries and a-half in which

Newfoundland has been in the possession of Europeans. But it is to be lamented that now, when we have taken up the cause of a barbarously treated people, so few should remain to reap the benefit of our plans for their civilization. The institution and its supporters will agree with me, that, after the unfortunate circumstances attending past encounters between the Europeans and the Red Indians, it is best now to employ Indians belonging to the other tribes to be the medium of beginning the intercourse we have in view; and indeed I have already chosen three of the most intelligent men from among the others met with in Newfoundland to follow up my search.

In conclusion, I congratulate the institution on the acquisition of several ingenious articles, the manufacture of the *Boeothicks*, some of which we had the good fortune to discover on our recent excursion;—models of their canoes, bows and arrows, spears of different kinds, &c. and also a complete dress worn by that people. Their mode of kindling fire is not only original, but as far as we at present know, is peculiar to the tribe. These articles, together with a short vocabulary of their language consisting of 200 to 300 words, which I have been enabled to collect, prove the Boeothicks to be a distinct tribe from any hitherto discovered in North America. One remarkable characteristic of their language, and in which it resembles those of Europe more than any other Indian languages do, with which we have had an opportunity of comparing it,—is its abounding in diphthongs. In my detailed report, I would propose to have plates of these articles, and also of the like articles used by other tribes of Indians, that a comparative idea may be formed of them; and, when the Indian

female *Shawnawdithit* arrives in St John's, I would recommend that a correct likeness of her be taken, and be preserved in the records of the institution. One of the specimens of mineralogy which we found in our excursion, was a block of what is called *Labrador Felspar*, nearly four one-half feet in length, by about three feet in breadth and thickness. This is the largest piece of that beautiful rock yet discovered any where. Our subsistence in the interior was entirely animal food, deer and beavers, which we shot.

*   *   *   *   *

"*Resolved*,—That the measures recommended in the president's report be agreed to; and that the three men, Indians of the Canadian and Mountaineer tribes, be placed upon the establishment of this institution, to be employed under the immediate direction and control of the president; and that they be allowed for their services such a sum of money as the president may consider a fair and reasonable compensation: That it be the endeavour of this institution to collect every useful information respecting the natural productions and resources of this island, and, from time to time, to publish the same in its reports: That the instruction of *Shawnawdithit* would be much accelerated by bringing her to St John's, &c.: That the proceedings of the institution, since its establishment, be laid before his Majesty's Secretary of State for the Colonial Department, by the president, on his arrival in England.

(Signed) "A.W. des BARRES,
Chairman and Vice-Patron."

The End

www.ingramcontent.com/pod-product-compliance
Lightning Source LLC
Chambersburg PA
CBHW060023300526
45794CB00003B/1270